TAKE TWO

A JOURNAL
FOR NEW BEGINNINGS

By Ellen Watson,
Kari Herer &
Kate Simpson

CHRONICLE BOOKS
SAN FRANCISCO

ISBN 978-1-4521-8054-0

Manufactured in China.

MIX
Paper from
responsible sources
FSC™ C136333

Design by **LIZZIE VAUGHAN** and **KATHERINE YAO**.

Page 17 quote: Pablo Neruda, Nobel Lecture, 1971 (© The Nobel Foundation). Reproduced with permission from the Nobel Foundation.

Page 28 quote: David Whyte, "The Well of Grief," from *River Flow: New & Selected Poems,* 2007 (© Many Rivers Press, Langley, WA, USA). Reproduced with permission from Many Rivers Press.

Page 164 quote: Miller Williams, "Compassion," from *The Ways We Touch: Poems,* 1997. Reproduced with permission from the University of Illinois Press.

10 9 8 7 6 5 4 3 2 1

Chronicle books and gifts are available at special quantity discounts to corporations, professional associations, literacy programs, and other organizations. For details and discount information, please contact our corporate/premiums department at corporatesales@chroniclebooks.com or at 1-800-759-0190.

Chronicle Books LLC
680 Second Street
San Francisco, CA 94107
www.chroniclebooks.com

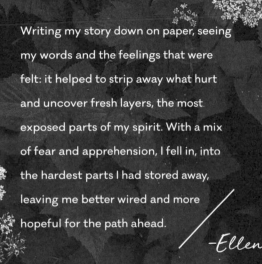

Writing my story down on paper, seeing
my words and the feelings that were
felt: it helped to strip away what hurt
and uncover fresh layers, the most
exposed parts of my spirit. With a mix
of fear and apprehension, I fell in, into
the hardest parts I had stored away,
leaving me better wired and more
hopeful for the path ahead.

—Ellen

Contents

WELCOME TO TAKE TWO 9

HOW TO USE THIS JOURNAL 12

I

Surviving Change 15

II

Building Your Inner World 53

III

Finding the Courage
to Move Forward 95

IV

Reconnecting 135

CONCLUSION 174

RESOURCES 177

SELECTED SOURCES 180

ABOUT US 190

Welcome to Take Two

IF YOU'RE READING THIS, perhaps you're seeking answers—answers to questions that are concrete or questions that are hazy. You've been through a transition, a change in emotional season, or you're experiencing loss and its overwhelming grief. Whatever the case, we're so glad you're here. Each of us, *every single one of us*, has been in that space. Off axis. Untethered. Or worse, knee deep in a sensation of feeling stuck—like molasses. In our pursuit of easier times, we often seek out methods for self-healing. We practice yoga; we meditate. We go to therapy and attend retreats that uncover a wellspring of tears. We ground ourselves in nature; we listen to podcasts. We focus on gratitude and try to envision better chapters to come. But what many of us have not done is journal in a way that feels actionable, using our words and other research-based tools to further our healing.

Neuroscientists used to believe that the brain's ability to change came to a halt when we were young. But in the latter part of the twentieth century, they discovered the concept of "neuroplasticity," finding that the adult brain is more malleable than previously thought, and that it's governed by neural pathways that become deepened by our habitual thoughts. We now know that when our brain defaults to the remembrance of feeling hurt or shame or emptiness—to that place of *not letting go*—we can choose to positively rewire it. Deepening the positive neural grooves in our brain helps us regulate our emotions, something we can do to live a longer, more peaceful life. Journaling can be a powerful tool for the cognitive healing of our own heart, literally forming new neural pathways, rendered simply with our hands.

Why? Because this practice helps to create resilience—that striking ability to encounter the elements of a storm whirling all around us and still turn our faces into the wind. It's an energetic allowance inside of us that, over time, empowers us to bravely capture the beautiful memories along with the unbearable sorrows. To begin to understand that perhaps this particular story isn't happening *to us*—but *for us*. To gather together all of the components that have shaped our life experience, build on that wisdom—whether welcome or unwelcome—and still move forward. And to know that this healing, this process of moving through hard times, doesn't end here: it's a continual, lifelong process. There is so much reward in the growth, in that redevelopment of who and where we have been, that filters into the human we aspire to be.

We are not therapists. We are women who have encountered trials of the living, breathing human condition. Here you'll find self-healing exercises in the form of writing prompts, as well as tools to help you move forward, to feel less fastened to fear. These are things we wish we'd explored when we fell on hard times. If something doesn't feel right or make sense for you, move on or come back to it later. If you're really struggling, there's no shame in seeking professional help. We all did—there are only so many friends' shoulders to cry on.

We're traveling this road together. Collectively, as humans, we've left copious amounts of emotional stuffing in our wake. Hard times abound for everyone, but it's these threads, these very chapters, that stitch us back together.

Clouds come floating into my life, no longer to carry rain or usher storm, but to add color to my sunset sky.

—RABINDRANATH TAGORE

11

How to Use This Journal

THIS JOURNAL IS FILLED WITH activities and writing prompts to help you write your own story. Bolstering one's resilience requires a healthy dose of self-awareness, a little grit to be able to perform an internal audit, and, in the case of this journal, a pen. Writing one's story—putting it down on paper—can be incredibly healing. So what does neuroscience have to do with this journal? Well, it's pretty simple.

Scientific research tells us that writing your story can change your brain.

Recent studies have shown that writing your story in a journal, even for just three days, can retrain thought patterns and *actually change how you feel*. This journal includes actionable tools that, according to current scientific research, help build resilience. Writing prompts that stem from the most current brain research help us deepen new neural pathways and offer us, in this journey, a self-propelled engine that puts us on the road to better emotional health. (Flip to the end of the journal to take a deeper dive into research sources.)

This journal uses the natural cycle of the four seasons as a guide to travel the arc of a stressful emotional event. Beginning with the slow withering of autumn, the journal moves through the dormancy of a cold winter and into the gradual regrowth of springtime. With the arrival of summer, we begin to reach a new normal. Each stage of the arc is considered a critical passage, and at times can feel complicated and challenging, but the research shows it can be difficult to get to the end without moving through each one. You'll find tools in each stage that have been proven to build resiliency, that ask you to go inward in order to build outward, offering ways that you can mine your story and write it into feelings, defining elements of the details—*of how you felt*—along the way.

It's in the writing, in these four sections of tools, that you may begin to feel the shift. Perhaps slowly, or perhaps as meteoric thoughts. This forward movement can sometimes feel fluid, traveling outward, inward, and then out again, like the circuitous path of a spiral found in nature.

So, this writing, this process? This is self-healing—and an opportunity to tell your story.

Surviving Change

Life has been going along at a reasonable clip. Routines are in place, the patterns of your life so deeply set. You drive the same metaphorical roads each day—and then it happens. The unforeseen. Perhaps it's sudden, or perhaps it arrives as a slow burn, like an autumn leaf, its edges ever so slightly beginning to curl, the height of its beauty only just passed. Somewhere in your landscape, there has been great change—perhaps in grieving the loss of a dream or expectation, or the loss of a loved one.

This experience—this new reality—can bring with it a vast array of emotional responses: profound grief, the wilds of fear, anxious bewilderment, or bouts of seething anger. Regardless of the reception, our resilience is being tested. This time may feel isolating or bring anxiety or depression. It feels like life as you once knew it continues on around you, but your world has come apart at the seams, a chasmal void left in its place.

We humans often wish to fast-forward to the next chapter, to find immediate gratification, perhaps latch onto a healing modality in hopes it will take the pain away. And sure, that might happen—but like a temporary bandage, it will only cover the wound for a short while. There is much to be gained

And we must
pass through
solitude and
difficulty,
isolation and
silence in order
to reach forth to
the enchanted
place where we
can dance our
clumsy dance
and sing our
sorrowful song.

—**PABLO NERUDA**

in the reality, and in the acceptance, of
sorrow. It may not be desired, pain and
suffering, but there are lessons to be
learned and new trails to blaze. Maybe
not today. Maybe today the ache and
the anguish feel like too much, and
that's when we suggest taking a break.
Be kind to yourself. After all, this is
an emotional crossing, and you get to
create the itinerary.

Journaling

Journaling is shown to be healing for both heart and mind. It might feel vulnerable to write things down, stirring up memories and emotions that are tied to grief, so we suggest keeping this journal somewhere that feels safe, somewhere private. This is your writing and, ultimately, a personal endeavor you are undertaking in the process of self-healing. In this section, we guide you through five prompts designed to lead you into your writing in a way that is restorative.

HOW DO I START?

Start where you are.

Owning our story and loving ourselves through that process is the bravest thing that we will ever do.

—BRENÉ BROWN

We encourage you, before each writing exercise, to take three deep breaths into your belly. It's scientifically proven to help you feel calmer, more centered, and more present.

Begin with something easy—just start writing, and see what begins to unfold. Jot down a few sentences about your day or about a specific conversation that happened earlier. The details don't actually matter here, but putting pen to paper does. It's like jumping rope before a strenuous workout, some quick wind sprints for your emotional spirit.

I went through a door
and when I went to go
back out, it was gone.
There was no way to get
back to the life I had led.
Everything had changed.
Whatever opens us is
never as important as
what it opens.

—MARK NEPO

How do you feel in your body? What are the actual
sensations you are experiencing as you observe this
blank page? Write about how you feel *right now.*

The Well of Grief

Those who will not slip beneath
    the still surface on the well of grief,

turning down through its black water
    to the place we cannot breathe,

will never know the source from which we drink,
    the secret water, cold and clear,

nor find in the darkness glimmering,
    the small round coins,
        thrown by those who wished for something else.

—DAVID WHYTE

Now that you've begun to work on writing how you feel, start to write your story, the one that brought you to this journal. Try to focus on the basics: What time of year did this particular chapter begin? Who was there? What did they say or do, and what did you say or do in response?

Autumn

The leaves fall, fall as from far,

Like distant gardens withered in the heavens;

They fall with slow and lingering descent.

And in the nights the heavy Earth, too, falls

From out the stars into the Solitude.

Thus all doth fall. This hand of mine must fall

And lo! the other one:—it is the law.

But there is One who holds this falling

Infinitely softly in His hands.

—RAINER MARIA RILKE

Looking back at what you've written, try to name the emotions you were experiencing. Label them, and write about each one. Do you feel any distance from the intensity of the feeling?

At times, the world around us can feel cinematic + caustic, but we learn, through the deepest wounds, through those times of afflictive emotional injury, that our well-being comes from being. And that we need to be a brave + mighty presence during the mess—because this is living out loud, and there is compellingly deep connection in the truth. It's only in this being, this truth telling—this mash-up of who we were in our past and who we think, who we hope we'll be—that we are able to capture the rawness, the beauty of this real + heartfelt life.

—Ellen

Think about how your story fits into the bigger context of your life. Has it changed your perspective? Are there elements you value differently now or no longer take for granted?

Building Your Inner World

Reality has begun to set in, so here we take a deep dive into tools of self-care and exploration. Just as daylight diminishes in the depths of winter and we tend to burrow, perhaps becoming less social, we go inward during this emotional work, like a hibernal tree when its leaves go dormant before a spring bloom. In this section, we invite you—and this part can be tricky— to sit with your feelings. In the same way that regrowth found in nature requires quiet reconstruction, our own mind and consciousness must travel inward before we can begin to rebuild our outward self. This is important work, allowing us to probe deeper into the why, to examine how things happened the way they did, while also gracefully letting those experiences sink in, perhaps reaffirming that these shifts are not happening *to* you, but for the greater good of the future you. So allow yourself to carve out some space, some time to recalibrate. Allow yourself this time to heal.

As you begin to explore your feelings more deeply through self-reflection, try not to get caught in the spiral of negative self-talk. Current brain research explains to us how "neurons that fire together, wire together"—meaning that self-defeating thoughts and actions only deepen gloomy neural grooves, causing them to feel *even gloomier*. See what we're getting at here? The same principle works in reverse: Focus on the positive in your life, and you'll train your neural pathways to home in more closely on optimism and good energy. Let's coach our own brains, and ultimately our hearts, toward a more promising path: one of acceptance, self-love, and a greater sense of contentment.

If we had no winter, the spring would not be so pleasant.

—ANNE BRADSTREET

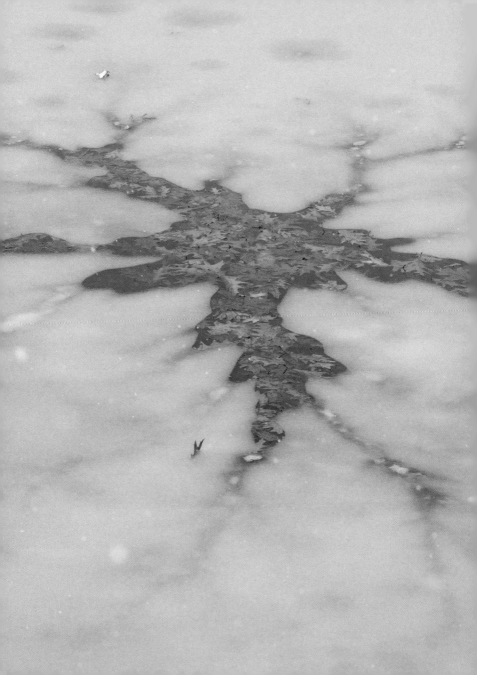

Mindfulness
Self-Compassion
Gratitude

These are the three essential
tools that can offer helpful support
in this process of self-reflection
and self-healing.

Each one helps us
revisit the course of a
spiral in nature, rein-
forcing the notion that
one must go inward,
really venture through
the darkness, to get to
the lighter days—and
sentiments—of spring.

It's this deep dive, the
emotional notetaking
and observation of how
you are feeling, that
lays the groundwork for
self-compassion and
gratitude as you begin to
rebuild the more outer
realms of your life. Even
better, research tells us that
utilizing these tools can
actually assist in the healthy
rewiring of your brain.

How do we start to notice what we're thinking and feeling?

We need to create some space—
to take a pause—
so we can observe but also monitor the emotions we are experiencing.

Research professors Brené Brown and Kristin Neff use the term "courageous presence" as a way to think about mindfulness, because it takes grit to stay present in a specific moment when you are facing difficult emotions. Noticing feelings and sensations that are in our orbit, that flit in and out of our brains, is a mighty task. But to be mindful of these conditions, without judgment, leads to important growth because this begins to train our brains to focus more on the present moment. It's been scientifically shown that practicing mindfulness for ten minutes a day for thirty days supports increased positive emotions, reduces stress, and increases self-compassion. For some, its benefits can be felt with only a few days of practice.

> Only when you drink from the river of silence shall you indeed sing. And when you have reached the mountain-top, then you shall begin to climb. And when the earth shall claim your limbs, then shall you truly dance.
>
> —KHALIL GIBRAN, *THE PROPHET*

SELF-COMPASSION

What happens when we experience strong emotions and critical internal conversations?

Offering ourselves some compassion—just as we would for a friend—can begin to soften the edges of a challenging time, offering us agency and perhaps more readiness for what lies around the next corner. This does not mean our injury has healed, but that we can find greater self-compassion for who and where we are, having gone through this difficult emotional season.

Feeling thankful for things that are going right or for supportive friends and family: These are things that can bring on a sense of gratitude.

But we can also train our minds to be grateful for the small moments: the warmth of a cup of tea in our hands or the smell of freshly cut flowers.

Try to hold on to these impressions for twenty to thirty seconds. Documenting specific reflections of our day, snippets of time for which we feel thankful, helps to retrain our brain and deepen our positive neural pathways. Current research shows that writing down three things you are grateful for every day for twenty-one days significantly increases your level of optimism, the benefits lasting for up to six months. We include a place for you to do this at the end of this section.

Put your hand over your heart, take a deep breath, and accept where you are precisely at this moment. Using the instructions given in "Mindfulness: How to Get Started" (facing page) set a timer for five minutes and give it a try. Even the most experienced mindfulness practitioner can be bombarded with thoughts. This is where "retraining" your thoughts begins, and it gets easier with practice. Once you're done, write about what thoughts came up for you. Were there any surprising emotions that arose?

MINDFULNESS: HOW TO GET STARTED

Sit quietly and focus on your natural breathing. Listen to the inhale and exhale of your breath. As other thoughts begin to roll in, gently notice "I'm thinking" and direct your attention back to your breathing. If you notice any emotions coming up for you, allow them to be present without judgment. If sitting in silence feels too difficult, seek out some free guided meditations online—see the Resources section (page 177) for a few suggestions.

During times of anxiety or grief, I often find myself looking to the trees. Whether full of foliage or stripped bare of leaves, a glimpse of nature always compels me to redirect my lens to the here and now— because the fullness of life is still happening all around me.

—Ellen

We often find our mind ruminating on stories we tell ourselves—
about why people act the way they do, how they hurt us, or how
they've let us down. These stories often follow us around through
life, getting in the way of our relationships with others—and with
ourselves. And yet, do we really know, as fact, that all parts of
this story are true? What happens when we question the truth of
the assumptions and judgments we're making? Does it change
our perspective and, thus, our response? Write about a situation
that has been looping in your mind for some time, focusing on a
piece of the story that *might* not be true.

Our capacity to
live fully, wakeful,
lovingly is intrinsically
intertwined with how
we relate to changes
that happen; losses
in our life . . . whether
we face that reality,
whether we open to it,
whether we're present
with it, or whether
something in us keeps
it as a story.

—TARA BRACH

Close your eyes and imagine an older, wiser, all-loving you.
What kind-hearted words could that person communicate
to you? Write a letter to yourself in that same voice,
offering compassionate advice.

No one can see their reflection in running water.

It is only in still water that we can see.

—TAOIST PROVERB

Write down three changes you can make—right now—
that would show yourself some compassion during this
time in your life.

When we're in a state of self-compassion, we are in a state of loving, connected presence. When we evoke that state, every time there's pain or failure or mistakes or struggle, we aren't defined anymore by those negative emotions.

—KRISTIN NEFF

Write down three things you're grateful for every day for
twenty-one days. Let them be small moments from your day,
brief impressions for which you are thankful. Try to observe
and identify how this practice makes you feel.

DAY ONE

DAY TWO

DAY THREE

DAY FOUR

DAY FIVE

DAY SIX

DAY SEVEN

DAY EIGHT

DAY NINE

DAY TEN

DAY ELEVEN

DAY TWELVE

DAY THIRTEEN

DAY FOURTEEN

DAY FIFTEEN

DAY SIXTEEN

DAY SEVENTEEN

DAY EIGHTEEN

DAY NINETEEN

DAY TWENTY

DAY TWENTY-ONE

Finding the Courage to Move Forward

Building on the work we've done on the inside—the steady presence and reflection, as well as the honoring and acknowledging of the emotional travels we've taken—this next section helps us step out of that darkness and back into our days and into our communities with slightly firmer footing. We are trying to build something new, something different, like the unfurling of a tender bloom in the spring, a time where longer days translate to more sunlight, *and* perhaps more lightness of being. This is a good time to begin planting seeds of renewal all around you. A new life chapter isn't always easy; change and grief can bring fragility and a raw vulnerability that asks us to really turn our faces into the wind, into the elements heading our way. But as we become more conscious of the rebuilding, of our work taking root, we can also take this opportunity to realize this is the start of something fresh. This sowing of seeds: it is a new beginning. A regeneration.

This leads to the next question: *Which seeds do we want to plant?* Let's cultivate an overall vision for our lives moving forward, focusing our life lens on constructive and forward-thinking feelings and the components that will help us to feel better, not worse. Visualizing a future that concentrates on positive emotional aspirations, not material goods, is key here, as the research shows the latter simply doesn't make us happier over the long term.

They tried to bury us.

They didn't know we were seeds.

—MEXICAN PROVERB

To get to this starting point, we need to take inventory and identify our biggest roadblocks in the process of moving forward. Whether it's our own self-limiting language, the stories we tell and then retell ourselves, or external forces in our orbit, research shows that the lens through which we perceive and process emotions has great significance. This lens is called *mind-set*, and it has tremendous impact on outcome—*any outcome*. Our mindset encapsulates our attitude, our behaviors, and the parts of our innermost self, and it is scientifically proven to have an effect on the body and how it reacts— because when we believe something as truth, it alters the biochemicals in our brain and changes how we feel.

Mindset

The following prompts help us identify how we'd like our life to look—both today and in the future—as well as what's holding us back. By shining a light on our own self-limiting beliefs, while also questioning their truth, we have the opportunity to reframe these thoughts into a positive mindset, which will deepen new neural grooves. As we learn to fine-tune and modify our mindset, the lens through which we view our lives, we can move closer to the life we want.

It's natural to go down the road of negative self-talk. It's like stepping out my door for a run, taking a left out the driveway, always taking the same route. Living a purposeful life is a daily recommitment, choosing to focus on the positive and, on some days, to hang a right, to take in new sights while quieting the timeworn and critical voices of my past.

—Ellen

SETTING A VISION

Take some time to contemplate what lies ahead. What are you seeking most deeply in your life? Try not to focus on material outcomes (such as "I'd like a new car"); studies show this won't make us happier in the long run. Instead, try to dig deeper into the work of self-reflection you've done here in this journal; think about what it is that both your heart and mind profoundly desire. Get specific, and define your vision—what you are seeking today, next month, and next year—with the most optimistic elements you can capture.

TODAY

NEXT MONTH

NEXT YEAR

To achieve your life vision, how you'd like your life to look and feel, you have to be aware of what's holding you back. Quite often, there are deep-rooted beliefs standing in our way—we doubt ourselves, fear failure, believe we can't do it. What kinds of roadblocks are getting in your way? Name these obstacles, both internal and external, here.

If you can get tuned into your inner compass, if you can really listen in to these internal sensations and get through the rigidity of fixed ideas, if you can find your way, there's often this beautiful flowering of harmony in the vision of where you can go. The beautiful thing about being a human being is you have choice.

—DAN SIEGEL

Reflect on the internal roadblocks you just listed. Negative self-talk often acts as cinder blocks tied to our dreams, anchoring us to a place of being unable to make change. These often become habitual thoughts that you tell yourself—but they are just stories. When we're able to see them for what they are, we can choose not to listen. Write down three self-limiting beliefs that are holding you back.

ONE

TWO

THREE

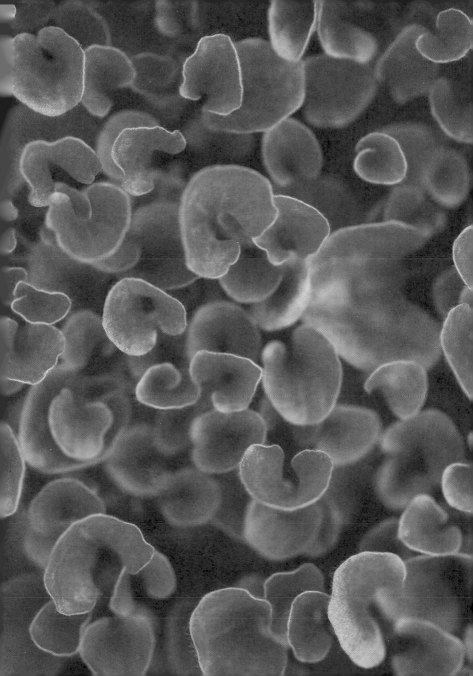

Take each story—each limiting belief—you've listed and reframe it as a positive affirmation. For example, "I'm not good enough" can be rewritten as "I can achieve whatever I set my mind to." Or "I'm unlovable" is replaced with "I am worthy and deserve to be loved."

ONE

TWO

Be mindful of intention.
Intention is the seed that
creates our future.

—BUDDHIST PROVERB

THREE

Calming Breath Exercise

This breath exercise can help you to feel calmer.

1 Exhale completely through your mouth, while making a deep sighing sound.

2 While counting to four, close your mouth and inhale quietly through your nose.

3 Hold your breath for several seconds.

4 Slowly exhale completely through your mouth, while making the same sighing sound.

5 Now inhale again and repeat the cycle three more times.

Being mindful of the self-limiting beliefs you've just listed, and the negative influence they can have on your vision, think about concrete steps you can take to nurture the elements of how you would like your life to look. What actions can you take to cultivate these seeds as they develop and grow?

Our minds actually change reality. In other words, the reality we will experience tomorrow is in part a product of the mindset we hold today.

—ALIA CRUM

List three specific things you can do today,
next week, and next month:

TODAY

NEXT WEEK

NEXT·MONTH

Reconnecting

In this final section of the journal, we gather up the tools and writing we've worked through in the previous three sections, adding some last crucial items to our toolbox. The work you've accomplished within these pages has taken you on a broad and complex arc, but now that the seeds have been planted, you may find yourself feeling ready to take courageous steps forward. The research shows that connecting with the people around us, with compassion, is instrumental to our emotional health and an important catalyst for self-healing. These first steps may be tentative, as there are still elements of what happened that will permeate your spirit, perhaps frequently. And that's OK. We can honor those emotions, observe them for what they are, and still move forward. Using the exercises you have discovered throughout this journal, try to allow yourself and this new chapter to unfold. Like a colorful bloom discovered in the wilds of nature, there is both beauty and grace to be found in regrowth.

With this recognition—this deep dive you've taken into your internal world—you may find you possess a new awareness of your surroundings. Your outer world may look a little different, as the personal periscope of this work begins to surface.

> No matter
> how tall the
> mountain is, it
> cannot block
> the sun.
>
> —CHINESE
> PROVERB

Your circle of friends may have changed, or perhaps the constructs of your village, your people, have left you feeling disconnected. This isn't uncommon— feeling you can't relate as closely, that you don't fit in as you once did. And yet connection is critical to our well-being. Research tells us this—that the combination of high-quality personal relationships and hearty, face-to-face community support makes for better health, both physically and psychologically. Feeling connected to others—with a sense of inclusion—helps our nervous systems to experience lower stress levels, which contributes to overall contentment and long-term happiness. Connection can obviously be felt with close family and friends but also within collective social groups such as a local book club or running group, community volunteer work, or a supportive faith-based circle. Being part of something bigger, helping others, forming relationships with other humans, live and in person—these require stepping outside of our comfort zones. They call for vulnerability, and they are sometimes hard to do. But again, when we put ourselves out there, deepening positive—and peaceful—neural grooves, we're teaching our brains and our hearts how to better regulate emotions, which we now know is the key to a long, happy life.

And the day came when the risk to remain tight in a bud was more painful than the risk it took to blossom.

—ELIZABETH APPELL

Compassion

Compassion is an emotional response to someone's suffering along with the desire or urge to lessen it. Compassion is different from empathy, in which we try to understand another person's feelings but don't have a compelling urge to help.

Cultivating compassion is an essential task that connects us to those with whom we are closest, as well as throughout our broader community.

Why? Because they, too, are learning difficult lessons along the way.

Research has found that a compassion practice rewires our brain circuitry, strengthening positive neural grooves and creating better, more healthful behavioral patterns. So as you come into contact with others, try to pause. Take a deep mindful breath, sit with the experience for a moment, and remember that *each and every one of us has a story—* full of love and joy, pain and sorrow.

The following journal prompts will guide you through some compassion-oriented exercises, asking you to observe those around you, perhaps softening toward those who may have hurt you.

> Compassion recognizes the suffering of another as a reflection of our own pain: "I understand this; I suffer the same way." Compassion is shared suffering.
>
> —JACK KORNFIELD

As we journey forward and continue to build on this—fostering compassionate feelings for others—we are creating a compelling framework for a life well lived.

ONE IMPORTANT TIP: Having compassion for others is not the same as welcoming them into your personal fold. We can feel soft-hearted toward people despite knowing they're not safe to be a part of our tribe. It's totally OK—and necessary—to create boundaries; they serve as a crucial reminder that we simply cannot be all things to all people, and we don't have to invite everyone close.

Think about two or three people already in your life with whom you'd like to deepen a friendship or relationship. They can be part of your everyday circle or someone who feels a little too distant or perhaps exists on the periphery. How can you deepen these relationships? List some specific actions you can take to connect with each one.

Being a part of this equation, it takes a little grit. Some determination. But there's no actual cost, unless you count the opening of your heart and the rising numbers of your village. Unfurl those closed fists, outstretch your hands that know so well how to hold, and pull your people in. The rewards are there for you, patiently waiting.

—Ellen

Think about someone you came into contact with yesterday or today. Try to envision the details of their face, and let your mind wander toward the different types of struggles they may have endured. List them here.

Think of a specific act of kindness you can undertake for three
people in your life—offering a smile to someone who looks
a little down, bringing a delicious meal to a friend, or lending
someone in need a helping hand. Name each act here, and put
a check mark next to it when completed. Then, write about how
the act of helping someone made you feel.

ONE

TWO

THREE

This prompt may feel hard, but developing compassion for those who have hurt us will settle our hearts and help us move on.

Think of someone who has hurt you emotionally, who has wronged you in some way. This can be anyone you choose—if you are not ready, don't force yourself. But see if you can push aside any negative feelings for a minute. Think of possible ways they may have suffered during their life—perhaps from a difficult childhood, past hurtful relationships, or a deep lack of self-worth. Try to summon a small glimmer of compassion for this person and their suffering, and write about it here.

Compassion

Have compassion for everyone you
meet, even if they don't want it. What
seems conceit, bad manners, or cyni-
cism is always a sign of things no ears
have heard, no eyes have seen. You do
not know what wars are going on down
there where the spirit meets the bone.

—MILLER WILLIAMS

Sit quietly for a moment, take a deep breath in and out, and think of all the people in the world who are suffering in the same way you are. There is extraordinary power in knowing we're not alone in our suffering, that we are all on this journey together. Write about the ways we collectively struggle.

SECTION IV • RECONNECTING

170

Conclusion

AND, SO, HERE WE ARE. The end of *Take Two*. Sit with that notion for a moment to process that sentiment and the body of work you have completed throughout these four sections. In shoring up your resilience, you have explored the many seasons of self-renewal. You've learned about and utilized research-proven tools that promote positive neural grooves in your brain. You've carried out important internal work along the way, and you've begun to set sights on the larger community around you—your outer world. This journal has taught you critical tools, such as restorative writing; the practice of mindfulness, gratitude, and self-compassion; noticing your mindset; and the art of compassion in the honoring of others. You have armed yourself—and your brain—with indispensable skills for self-healing.

This is important because your work will continue to be a process, like a spiral in nature that journeys outward, determinedly and with confidence, only to shrink back to center, slightly drained and depleted, to a place we have already been. There will be good days, and also times that threaten to derail us, sending us off course. But you are now equipped with a supportive practice—a blueprint with actionable tools for a happier, more courageous heart and far better emotional health.

So let this steep, the culmination of writing and activities throughout this journal; let the work sink down into your cellular layers—and let it live there.

> Don't let yesterday use up too much of today.
>
> —PROVERB

RESOURCES

Words of wisdom. Podcasts that inspire. People we admire.

This is not a wholly comprehensive list, as the list of what's out there is staggeringly expansive, but the *Take Two* website (taketwojournal.com) includes active links to each resource, as well as a blog that highlights new research, podcasts, books, and talks we haven't included here.

Books

Brach, Tara. *True Refuge: Finding Peace and Freedom in Your Own Awakened Heart.* New York: Bantam Books, 2016.

Brown, Brené. *Braving the Wilderness: The Quest for True Belonging and the Courage to Stand Alone.* New York: Random House, 2017.

Brown, Brené. *Rising Strong: How the Ability to Reset Transforms the Way We Live, Love, Parent, and Lead.* New York: Random House, 2017.

Buettner, Dan. *Blue Zones of Happiness: Discovering the Secrets of the World's Happiest Places.* Washington, D.C.: National Geographic Society, 2017.

Chödrön, Pema. *When Things Fall Apart: Heart Advice for Difficult Times.* London: Thorsons Classics, 2017.

Greenberg, Melanie. *The Stress-Proof Brain: Master Your Emotional Response to Stress Using Mindfulness & Neuroplasticity.* Oakland, CA: New Harbinger Publications, 2016.

Hanson, Rick. *Hardwiring Happiness: The New Brain Science of Contentment, Calm, and Confidence.* New York: Harmony Books, 2016.

Kabat-Zinn, Jon. *Wherever You Go, There You Are: Mindfulness Meditation in Everyday Life.* New York: Hachette Books, 2014.

Kornfield, Jack. *A Lamp in the Darkness: Illuminating the Path through Difficult Times.* Boulder: Sounds True, 2014.

Lesser, Elizabeth. *Broken Open: How Difficult Times Can Help Us Grow.* New York: Villard, 2005.

Neff, Kristin. *Self-Compassion: The Proven Power of Being Kind to Yourself.* New York: William Morrow, an imprint of HarperCollins Publishers, 2011.

Neff, Kristin, and Christopher K. Germer. *The Mindful Self-Compassion Workbook: A Proven Way to Accept Yourself, Build Inner Strength, and Thrive.* New York: Guilford Press, 2018.

Podcasts

10% Happier with Dan Harris

Being Well with Dr. Rick Hanson and Forrest Hanson

The One You Feed

Oprah's SuperSoul Conversations

The Science of Happiness

Therapist Uncensored Podcast

Tara Brach

Untangle, the podcast from Meditation Studio

Apps

Insight Timer: Free app with guided meditations on a number of top-
ics (sleep help, relaxation, anxiety) as well as free meditation
instruction

Oprah & Deepak's Twenty-One-Day Meditation Experience: Available for
free three times a year (available for purchase anytime)

TED Talks / YouTube Videos

TED Talk: "Change Your Mindset, Change the Game" by Dr. Alia Crum

TED Talk: "How Meditation Can Reshape Our Brains" by Dr. Sara Lazar

TED Talk: "Listening to Shame" by Dr. Brené Brown

TED Talk: "The Power & Science of Social Connection" by Dr. Emma
Seppälä

TED Talk: "The Power of Vulnerability" by Dr. Brené Brown

YouTube: "Neuroplasticity" by Sentis; two-minute visual explanation of
neuroplasticity

Websites

Kristin Neff: www.self-compassion.org (Includes free guided meditations)

Mindful Awareness Research Center at UCLA: www.uclahealth.org/marc

Greater Good Science Center at UC Berkeley: www.greatergood.berkeley.edu

SELECTED SOURCES

Organized by Tool

Emotionally Expressive Journaling

Baikie, Karen A., and Kay Wilhelm. "Emotional and Physical Health Benefits of Expressive Writing." *Advances in Psychiatric Treatment* 11, no. 5 (September 5, 2005): 338–346. apt.rcpsych.org/content/11/5/338.full.

Gortner, Eva-Maria, et al. "Benefits of Expressive Writing in Lowering Rumination and Depressive Symptoms." *Behavior Therapy* 37, no. 3 (2006): 292–303. doi:10.1016/j.beth.2006.01.004.

Hamby, Sherry. "Resilience and . . . 4 Benefits to Sharing Your Story." Psychology Today (September 3, 2013). www.psychologytoday.com/blog/the-web-violence/201309/resilience-and-4-benefits-sharing-your-story.

Harvard Health Publishing. "Writing about Emotions May Ease Stress and Trauma - Harvard Health." *Harvard Health Blog* (n.d.), www. health.harvard.edu/healthbeat/writing-about-emotions-may-ease-stress-and-trauma.

Pennebaker, James W., and John Frank Evans. *Expressive Writing: Words That Heal: Using Expressive Writing to Overcome Traumas and Emotional Upheavals, Resolve Issues, Improve Health, and Build Resilience.* Enumclaw, WA: Idyll Arbor, 2014.

Torre, Jared B., and Matthew D. Lieberman. "Putting Feelings Into Words: Affect Labeling as Implicit Emotion Regulation." *Emotion Review* 10, no. 2 (2018): 116–124. doi:10.1177/1754073917742706.

Deep Breathing

"Breathing: The Little Known Secret to Peace of Mind." *Psychology Today* (n.d.), www.psychologytoday.com/us/blog/feeling-it/201304 /breathing-the-little-known-secret-peace-mind.

Philippot, Pierre, et al. "Respiratory Feedback in the Generation of Emotion." *Cognition and Emotion* 16, no. 5 (2002): 605–627. doi:10.1080/02699930143000392.

Sarkar, Anjali A. "Functional Correlation between Breathing and Emotional States." *MOJ Anatomy & Physiology* 3, no. 5 (2017). doi:10.15406/mojap.2017.03.00108.

Yackle, Kevin, et al "Breathing Control Center Neurons That Promote Arousal in Mice." *Science* 355, no. 6332 (March 31, 2017): 1411–1415. science.sciencemag.org/content/355/6332/1411 /tab-figures-data.

Neuroplasticity

Doidge, Norman, MD. *The Brain That Changes Itself*. Melbourne, Australia: Scribe, 2010.

Greenberg, Melanie. *The Stress-Proof Brain: Master Your Emotional Response to Stress Using Mindfulness and Neuroplasticity*. Oakland, CA: New Harbinger, 2017.

Hebb, Donald Olding. *The Organization of Behavior: A Neuropsychological Theory*. New York: Wiley, 1949.

Helmstetter, Shad, PhD *The Power of Neuroplasticity*. Scotts Valley, CA: CreateSpace Independent Publishing Platform, 2014.

Kaschka, W. P., and M. Jandl. "How Can We Utilize Neuroplasticity to Overcome Treatment-Resistant Depression." *Journal of Affective Disorders* 107 (March 2008): S68–S69. doi.org/10.1016 /j.jad.2007.12.038.

Taylor, Jill Bolte, PhD *My Stroke of Insight: A Brain Scientist's Personal Journey*. London: Hodder & Stoughton, 2009.

Mindfulness

Bialylew, Elise. "This Is Exactly How Long You Need to Meditate to Feel the Benefits." *Thrive Global* (June 27, 2018). www.thriveglobal.com /stories/25175-meditate-to-feel-the-benefits.

Davidson, Richard J., PhD., et al. "Alterations in Brain and Immune Function Produced by. . . Psychosomatic Medicine." *Psychosomatic Medicine* 65, no. 4 (July 2003): 564–570. journals.lww.com /psychosomaticmedicine/Abstract/2003/07000/Alterations _in_Brain_and_Immune_Function_Produced.14.aspx. doi: 10.1097/01.PSY.0000077505.67574.E3.

Kabat-Zinn, Jon. "A Study in Happiness—Meditation, the Brain, and the Immune System." *Mindfulness* 9, no. 5 (2018): 1664–1667. doi:10.1007/s12671-018-0991-3.

Lutterveld, Remko Van, et al. "Meditation Is Associated with Increased Brain Network Integration." *NeuroImage* 158 (2017): 18–25. doi:10.1016/j.neuroimage.2017.06.071.

Powell, Alvin. "Harvard Researchers Study How Mindfulness May Change the Brain in Depressed Patients." *Harvard Gazette* (August 27, 2018). news.harvard.edu/gazette/story/2018/04/harvard-researchers-study-how-mindfulness-may-change-the-brain-in -depressed-patients/.

Seppälä, Emma M., PhD. "20 Scientific Reasons to Start Meditating Today." *Psychology Today* (September 11, 2013). www.psychologytoday. com/us/blog/feeling-it/201309/20-scientific-reasons-start -meditating-today.

Seppälä, Emma M., Jack B. Nitschke, Dana L. Tudorascu, Andrea Hayes, Michael R. Goldstein, Dong T. H. Nguyen, David Perlman, and Richard J. Davidson. "Breathing-Based Meditation Decreases Posttraumatic Stress Disorder Symptoms in U.S. Military Veterans: A Randomized Controlled Longitudinal Study." *Journal of Traumatic Stress* 27, no. 4 (August 2014): 397–405. doi:10.1002/jts.21936.

Self-Compassion

Arimitsu, Kohki, and Stefan G. Hofmann. "Effects of Compassionate Thinking on Negative Emotions." *Cognition and Emotion* 31, no. 1 (September 2015): 160–67. doi:10.1080/02699931.2015.1078292.

Ehret, Anna M., Jutta Joormann, and Matthias Berking. "Examining Risk and Resilience Factors for Depression: The Role of Self-Criticism and Self-Compassion." *Cognition and Emotion* 29, no. 8 (December 2014): 1496–504. doi:10.1080/02699931.2014.992394.

Marshall, Emma-Jane, and Robert N. Brockman. "The Relationships Between Psychological Flexibility, Self-Compassion, and Emotional Well-Being." *Journal of Cognitive Psychotherapy* 30, no. 1 (2016): 60–72. doi:10.1891/0889-8391.30.1.60.

Neff, Kristin D. "Self-Compassion and Psychological Well-Being." *PsycEXTRA Dataset* (2005). doi:10.1037/e633942013-240.

Samaie, Gh., and H. A. Farahani. "Self-Compassion as a Moderator of the Relationship between Rumination, Self-Reflection, and Stress." *Procedia - Social and Behavioral Sciences* 30 (2011): 978–82. doi:10.1016/j.sbspro.2011.10.190.

Gratitude

Achor, Shawn. "The Happiness Dividend." *Harvard Business Review* (July 23, 2014). hbr.org/2011/06/the-happiness-dividend.

Kini, P., et al. "The Effects of Gratitude Expression on Neural Activity." *NeuroImage* (March 2016). www.ncbi.nlm.nih.gov/pubmed/26746580.

Korb, Alex, PhD. "The Grateful Brain." *Psychology Today* (November 20, 2012). www.psychologytoday.com/us/blog/prefrontal-nudity/201211/the-grateful-brain.

Wong, Joel, and Joshua Brown. "How Gratitude Changes You and Your Brain." *Greater Good* (June 6, 2017). greatergood.berkeley.edu/article/item/how_gratitude_changes_you_and_your_brain.

Mindset

Crum, Alia J., et al. "Rethinking Stress: The Role of Mindsets in Determining the Stress Response." *Journal of Personality and Social Psychology* 104, no. 4 (2013): 716–733. doi:10.1037/a0031201.

Crum, Alia J., et al. "The Role of Stress Mindset in Shaping Cognitive, Emotional, and Physiological Responses to Challenging and Threatening Stress." *Anxiety, Stress, & Coping* 30, no. 4 (July 2017): 379–395. doi:10.1080/10615806.2016.1275585.

Jamieson, Jeremy P., et al. "Optimizing Stress Responses with Reappraisal and Mindset Interventions: An Integrated Model." *Anxiety, Stress, & Coping* 31, no. 3 (2018): 245–261. doi:10.1080/10615806.2018.1442615.

Park, Daeun, et al. "Beliefs About Stress Attenuate the Relation Among Adverse Life Events, Perceived Distress, and Self-Control." *Child Development* 89, no. 6 (May 2017): 2059–2069. doi:10.1111/cdev.12946.

Positive Affirmations

Cascio, Christopher N., Matthew Brook O'Donnell, Francis J. Tinney, Matthew D. Lieberman, Shelley E. Taylor, Victor J. Strecher, and Emily B. Falk. "Self-Affirmation Activates Brain Systems Associated with Self-Related Processing and Reward and Is Reinforced by Future Orientation." *Social Cognitive and Affective Neuroscience* 11, no. 4 (November 2015): 621–29. doi:10.1093/scan/nsv136.

Cohen, Geoffrey L., and David K. Sherman. "The Psychology of Change: Self-Affirmation and Social Psychological Intervention." *Annual Review of Psychology* 65, no. 1 (January 2014): 333–71. doi:10.1146/annurev-psych-010213-115137.

Dutcher, Janine M., J. David Creswell, Laura E. Pacilio, Peter R. Harris, William M. P. Klein, John M. Levine, Julienne E. Bower, Keely A. Muscatell, and Naomi I. Eisenberger. "Self-Affirmation Activates the Ventral Striatum." *Psychological Science* 27, no. 4 (February 2016): 455–66. doi:10.1177/0956797615625989.

Koole, Sander L., Karianne Smeets, Ad Van Knippenberg, and Ap Dijksterhuis. "The Cessation of Rumination Through Self-Affirmation." *Journal of Personality and Social Psychology* 77, no. 1 (1999): 111–25. doi:10.1037/0022-3514.77.1.111.

Compassion

Aknin, Lara B., and Elizabeth W. Dunn. "Wealth and Subjective Well-Being: Spending Money on Others Leads to Higher Happiness Than Spending on Yourself." In *Activities for Teaching Positive Psychology: A Guide for Instructors*, edited by J. J. Froh & A. C. Parks, 93–97. Washington, DC: American Psychological Association. doi:10.1037/14042-015.

Jazaieri, Hooria, Ihno A. Lee, Kelly Mcgonigal, Thupten Jinpa, James R. Doty, James J. Gross, and Philippe R. Goldin. "A Wandering Mind Is a Less Caring Mind: Daily Experience Sampling during Compassion Meditation Training." *Journal of Positive Psychology* 11, no. 1 (March 2015): 37–50. doi:10.1080/17439760.2015.1025418.

Klimecki, Olga M., and Tania Singer. "The Compassionate Brain." *Oxford Handbooks Online*, 10 (2017). doi:10.1093/oxfordhb /9780190464684.013.9.

Kok, Bethany E., Kimberly A. Coffey, Michael A. Cohn, Lahnna I. Catalino, Tanya Vacharkulksemsuk, Sara B. Algoe, Mary Brantley, and Barbara L. Fredrickson. "How Positive Emotions Build Physical Health." *Psychological Science* 24, no. 7 (May 2013): 1123–132. doi:10.1177/0956797612470827.

Seppälä, Emma, Emiliana Simon-Thomas, Stephanie L. Brown, Monica C. Worline, C. Daryl Cameron, and James R. Doty. *The Oxford Handbook of Compassion Science*. Oxford: Oxford University Press, 2017.

Weng, Helen Y., Andrew S. Fox, Alexander J. Shackman, Diane E. Stodola, Jessica Z. K. Caldwell, Matthew C. Olson, Gregory M. Rogers, and Richard J. Davidson. "Compassion Training Alters Altruism and Neural Responses to Suffering." *Psychological Science* 24, no. 7 (May 2013): 1171–180. doi:10.1177/0956797612469537.

Weng, Helen Y., Brianna Schuyler, and Richard J. Davidson. "The Impact of Compassion Meditation Training on the Brain and Prosocial Behavior." *Oxford Handbooks Online*, 10 (2017). doi:10.1093/oxfordhb/9780190464684.013.11.

Connection

Buettner, Dan. *The Blue Zones: Lessons for Living Longer from the People Who've Lived the Longest*. Washington, DC: National Geographic Society, 2009.

Ford, Brett Q., Julia O. Dmitrieva, Daniel Heller, Yulia Chentsova-Dutton, Igor Grossmann, Maya Tamir, Yukiko Uchida, Birgit Koopmann-Holm, Victoria A. Floerke, Meike Uhrig, Tatiana Bokhan, and Iris B. Mauss. "Culture Shapes Whether the Pursuit of Happiness Predicts Higher or Lower Well-being." *Journal of Experimental Psychology: General* 144, no. 6 (2015): 1053–062. doi:10.1037/xge0000108.

Lieberman, Matthew D. Social: *Why Our Brains Are Wired to Connect*. Oxford: Oxford University Press, 2015.

Porges, Stephen W. *The Polyvagal Theory: Neurophysiological Foundations of Emotions, Attachment, Communication, and Self-Regulation*. New York: Norton, 2011.

Porges, Stephen W. "Vagal Pathways." *Oxford Handbooks Online,* 10 (2017). doi:10.1093/oxfordhb/9780190464684.013.15.

Siegel, Daniel J. "Interpersonal Connection, Compassion, and Well-Being." In *Advances in Contemplative Psychotherapy,* edited by J. Loizzo, M. Neale, and E. Wolf, 118–30. New York: Routledge, 2017. doi:10.4324/9781315630045-11.

About Us

We are three women living in Maine, and mothers to seven children, combined. We are friends, offering support through the trials of life—through divorce, the challenges of parenting, the witnessing of a loved one suffering from illness, through loss and transition. Offering an ear, a good read, or a bad joke, we have shared deep-in-our-bones grief that simply can't be articulated, followed by bouts of medicinal laughter. Uncovering healing tools along the way, we sought help from numerous resources, but as we got caught up in our daily activities, these "instructions for life," the keys to getting back on our feet, quickly slipped away. So we decided to bring these elements all into one place, to gather research-proven science into a journal that aids with our own attempt to find balance. Our hope is that *Take Two* supports you, *supports all of us*, on a path to a thriving, more renewed life.

ELLEN WATSON, our writer, manages the social media strategy for a Maine-based nonprofit, and is a trained yoga teacher, freelance writer, and mom to two daughters.

KARI HERER is a commercial photographer who has collaborated on projects with companies such as Anthropologie, IKEA, and Restoration Hardware, has been a featured speaker at conferences worldwide, and is a mom to two daughters.

KATE SIMPSON, developer of the *Take Two* concept and format, is a consultant to a start-up in the impact investing field and mom to three kids.